How to see your
PRAYERS
be answered by
GOD!

How to see your
PRAYERS
be answered by
GOD!

PORSCHA DORSEY

XULON PRESS

Xulon Press
2301 Lucien Way #415
Maitland, FL 32751
407.339.4217
www.xulonpress.com

Unless otherwise indicated, Scripture quotations taken from the King James Version (KJV)–*public domain*.

Printed in the United States of America.

ISBN-13: 978-1-6312-9607-9

I want to introduce myself to the blessed person that's holding this book in their hands. My name is Porscha Dorsey and I was born and raised in Miami, Florida. From a young child my grandparents raised me and my wonderful sister. I am a mother of 5 amazing children and 1 amazing grandchild. My grandmother raised me and my sister in church which we attended Trinity Church in Miami. This book is about to explain how I became the woman that I am today because of PRAYER and building a relationship with God. I am an ordained Deaconess under the Pastors of Harry and Harriet McCain of New Direction Christian Center. My goal is to empower you to build and connect with God through prayer.

Deaconess Porscha

CONTENTS

Chapter One

THE TRANSITION EXPERIENCE...

When I begin to allow myself to go forward in God it's been a very hard journey and the reason I say that is because I have 5 children that had to go through this transition with me and it was difficult for them as well as myself. The reason I'm saying this is because I didn't raise my children in church like my grandmother did so when I finally found a church home to go to so that I can begin drawing closer to God, it was a tuff transformation because my children was asking many questions about my walk with God. But no matter what I kept pressing forward. As me and my children kept going to church and I've had a made up mind that it's time for us to be part of a church home. God has blessed us to be part of New Direction Christian Center and some amazing Pastor's. As I continued this journey and going to church and begin to read my bible my life was beginning to transform. The company of people begin to draw away and things I used to desire, I didn't desire anymore. I was at a point in my life where it didn't matter what it cost me because all I wanted was Jesus, I wanted to commit my life to the Lord and be saved. The closer my walk began to get with God, the more focused my children and I was adapting as well and that was encouraging me even more because I knew that I had to continue to go forward. I want to explain something, when you begin to grow in God and focus on your life and what's more important then you will see people and things change. But I want to encourage you who is reading this to continue your journey with God and allow His will to be done in your life. God knows the plans that He has for you (Jeremiah 29:11). Once you come out of your difficult moment because of transition, you will begin to realize that it was worth you pressing forward and pushing yourself to allow God to do whatever it is he's doing in your life. Anytime you commit yourself to do something that has to do with God, it will not be an easy sleigh. Trust the process and watch God show you that He is with you, allow the shift, it happened for me. When I became grounded in church then was my gift revealed that God instilled in me and that was PRAYER. I remember my first Lady asked me to pray for her over the phone and I was nervous because I never prayed to anyone and I didn't know what to say, but God begin to move in me and I was obedient so I went into prayer beginning to pray over the first Lady and just speak things that was powerful. The Holy Spirit began to take over and I was lost from my own self. When I stopped praying with her, she then said to me that I have a praying mantle on my life. At this time, I wasn't sure of what that meant because again this was my first time praying for somebody. But God has His way of bringing what is in you and out of you. As time, days, and months went on, I then was asked to start prayer in service before the Pastor bring the word of God. This was when God was really equipping me in my gift that was on the inside of me and that is PRAYER. The experience of my transition was worth it.

Chapter Two

SEEING THE MANIFESTATION...

I want you to know that my spiritual journey is not easy and throughout life we all on this earth will face mountains that we have to climb. Now, the more I pray to God and keep building with Him is the more I see Him answer my prayers. Remember the prayers that we witness God answer are those prayers that God see fit to be in line with His will so with that we can continue to Trust in God and not to lean on our own understanding.(Proverbs 3: 5-6). When you can see God move in your life that reassures us that He is hearing the prayers of the righteous.

Keep in mind that there is nothing to big for God to handle on our behalf. We must continue to press and pray and take God at His word because I've seen God over and over show Himself in my life because of my prayers and trust that I put in Him. I've faced some hardships in my time and when I needed comfort and peace, I cried out to God and I got before Him humbly as I knew how to and prayed! God is no respect of person. He will come through for you only if you will Trust Him in the middle of hard times. The enemy will do all he can to throw fireballs your way to distract your walk with God and cause you to stumble but all you need to do is hold on and keep your faith in God and know that He is Able. I'm saying all this because I've seen the hand of God on my Life and the manifestation of His power move because of my consistency in prayer. The bible tells us to go in your secret place and PRAY and when you do that you will find a peace and comfort because God will meet you there. The more you keep building a relationship with God the more you will see the manifestation of His glory in your life. I want to encourage you reader to keep praying and if things get a little more hectic then go on a fast and seek the Father because when it's an urgency, God will come through. As you continue to grow in your spiritual walk and read your bible so you can learn what the word says and how even others in the bible had trials and tribulations that they faced, but they knew God and had a firm relation-ship with Him. For instance we heard about the story of David who was a powerful King whom God chosen. Think about Moses who also was chosen by God to Lead the Israelites right, but remember they saw God's power in their life be manifested because of the rela-tionship and prayers that they presented to Him. Know that when we seek God and our hearts are in the right place, God will answer.

My prayer for you today is that you push forward and grow in God much as possible because God is always waiting on Us to call upon Him so He can come to our rescue as a father should. We are getting ready to experience life changing situations to happen in our life only if ewe seek the very heart of God, because He is that open door to our prayers being manifested in our life and in the lives of our love ones who we pray for on a daily basis. Each day that we wake up is already seeing God move because He makes the decision as to us being in the land of the living. Keep believing and trusting that God will because, God can.

Chapter Three

PUSHING THROUGH OBSTACLES...

*W*e all have had or are even now experiencing something in our life where it seems as though we can't climb over. But I'm here to tell you that God is Able no matter where you are or what you are facing, God can lift you right out. I know it's not as easy as it may sound when we are told to just pray to God or be strong and don't let things bother us. One thing I've learned in life is that we all have different situations and different results. We have children, husbands, wives and love ones that we pray for but yet are faced with hard times and we can encourage them as much as we can but at the end of the day they have to overcome their own obstacles in life. Just because we have challenges in life doesn't mean that we did something wrong or that God is mad at us. I say this because you would be surprised as to how many people live on thinking this way. But that's not the case. No one on earth is perfect and we will make mistakes on this journey called life but one thing is for sure is that we have temporary situations and there is an expiration date for our trial to be over with. I'm reminded of the word in the bible that says: Be strong in the Lord and by the power of His might (Ephesians 6:10). Remember everything that you're going through in life, God is with you and He is very concern about what we All face on this earth. Keep praying and seeking God for direction and guidance when you are in a hard situation because He is the only one that can and will show you how to react in your hardship. The obstacles we face with not stop coming but we can learn how to overcome in the midst of. I've faced some very difficult times in my life and one was concerning my son who I love dearly but I reached out to God in prayer and He gave me peace and restored my joy which activated my Trust and Faith in Him even the more. I've learned how to Push through my obstacles and strengthen myself in God knowing He is the finisher of my obstacles.

When you get to a place of a made up mind, then there is no situation that can consume you because you will have the ability to seek God and pray to Him about your concerns of life. When I'm faced with an hardship in my own life I go to my secret place and pray asking God to help me pull through, not to take me out of my situation but to help me get through my tuff situation. We have to trust and believe that God will answer ours prayers and that He hears us no matter what. God is faithful and he's caring because He understands what we go through on this earth. As long as we live on this earth, we will go through trails and face very difficult moments that seems so hard to deal with. I'm a witness to this and I can raise both arms up high to be the first to admit I have trials and I face difficult moments in my own personal life. But again, in order to see our problems drift away is by getting on your knees and reaching for the creator of this earth and that is Jehovah God almighty. Sometimes we all want to give up and throw in the towel but we shouldn't want to do that because we must learn how to face our mountains and climb them the best way we know how to and that's by PRAYING and watching God come through.

If the truth be told our tests and trials only comes to build us up and make us stronger. Listen, I've learned to take the bitter with the sweet and give my situations to God because he's the only one that can take your situation and make it work for your good but you don't give up and lose your trust and faith in God because everything we face in life has an expiration date. I want to only help you build your prayer life and become strong in your walk with God the father, Jesus and the holy spirit. Just keep in mind that hard times go come and go pretty much but there is always a strategy to everything.

Chapter Four

YOU WAS CHOSEN
FOR THE TASK...

*B*efore any of us was placed in our mother's womb, God knew us. With this being said God, hand picked who He needed to do His will on earth. Remember God pulls on who He see fit because He already knows all about US and He knows who will finish out the assignment that He places on our life. I want you to understand that when God wants to use you, it's because you are trusted by Him and that should mean a lot to you if you was chosen to do the will of the father. Don't get me wrong, everyone on the earth will not have a spiritual walk with God like others do to a certain measure but know that God loves US all the same no matter what. Some answers the call of God on their life but some don't because they think that you will have to live this "perfect" life which God already knows that we will have short comings and will continue to make human mistakes. But making mistakes doesn't discredit who you are as a person so don't take what I'm saying an confuse yourself. There is a scripture in the bible that tells Us that many are called but few are chosen! (Matthew 22:14). So this word is saying that God called many to come to Him and some answered, and the one's who answered was the one's whom He chose it's simple. One thing about God, He will not force nobody to come to Him, He will give you the opportunity to come. I thank God for calling many because I was one that answered and now I am chosen. My prayer is that you answer the call that's on your life. If you can sing, pray for others or even encourage people to the point that they are always calling on you to help solve their life issues, that is showing you that you are called to encourage and uplift people that's hurting or broken. That's a gift and God wants to take that gift and use it with everything in Him so that His glory can spread out upon the earth. One thing about God is that He doesn't share His glory He deserves all the credit from the person that He shapes and molds you to be. We are God's masterpiece and trophies when we are being used by Him. Pray that God stretch His hand towards you and touch you so that you can be used by Him, trust me you won't regret it because being chosen by Him is all that a person should want to long for. Be encouraged and keep praying to God and watch for yourself how He moves in your life as long as you have a willing heart to be changed and chosen by Him. The thing I did was started believing and trusting that

God will use my praying gift and strengthen me to pray for others and not just for myself. When we have been given a gift we can't be selfish with it because God will not be gloried that way so we must be mindful of our own selfish ways and think about others because God chose us for a task that we need to be focused on and know that whatever gift He placed on our life we need to perfect it. You and I was chosen to be a blessing.

Chapter Five

GOD DOESN'T
MAKE MISTAKES...

I want you to understand something. Everything that we face in our life rather it's good or bad, keep in mind that NOTHING catches our God in heaven by surprise and that's because He already knows the ends and outs of all our lives on this earth. There are some issues that we come up against is God's doing and He will test us to see how we will respond to situations all because He wants to build us to be strong and overcomers in Christ Jesus. Only God Himself knows what it takes for you and I to be all that we need to in this word in order to survive our hardships of life. When I'm faced with situations that's so difficult and frustrating at times I now just ask God to give me strength and guide me through. I've learned not to pray and ask God to take it away because He wants us to be able to walk in victory and be able to stand in the midst of hard times. When I think about my life for instance, my dad passed away when I was 12 yrs old, yes I was a little girl and then my mom 2 yrs later at the age of 14. I use you think about my childhood and question why did God take my parents at such a young age, even though my grandmother raised me but it's still a void of not having your biological parents around. I think at times how things would've been if they were still living. So in my case it had to happen for whatever reason God allowed it to. The bible says that All things work together for the GOOD of those that love God and who is called to His suppose (Romans 8: 28). This situation worked out for my good because God already called me from the womb of my mother and given me my gift of prayer. God truly doesn't make mistakes and He already know the beginning and the end of our life. I've been through some difficult situations growing up and I don't regret none of my hardships because God take what the devil meant for your bad into something good. Our mistakes only set us up to be strong and mighty in God. Never feel like what you've been through or going through in life now is a sign of punishment or God is upset... No, that's not the case, keep in mind that God want the best for Us, His sons and daughters. Continue to get on your knees at any given time you feel the need to talk to God the father. Whatever you might be facing at this particular time you're reading this book just remember I told you that everything we face in life, God never makes mistakes. Nothing surprises God... nothing!

When you decide to lean on God for His strength you will then see how He loves us in spite of our faults and flaws as to why we face difficult times. I'm thankful that God is our strong tower and way maker. All mistakes we've made helped us to be better people. Some people don't realize that God will keep you in perfect peace even in the midst of turbulence that took place. One thing about our keeper is that He will pull you through no matter what. Know God for yourself and trust that if He can't allow us to go through a tuff situation then how will we be able to grow spiritually. Just trust God.

Chapter Six

KEEPING YOUR FOCUS...

The most important thing in life is to be focused on yourself but not in a selfish way, no I'm not saying it like that but what I am saying to you and myself as well is that we need to always take time out for ourselves. The enemy will try any and everything to distract us from our focus because he knows that when we are alert and pay close attention to what God has placed in front of us, he knows there is NO stopping the process. Move forward into what God is directing you to do and how would you know that God is directing you to do something is by paying attention to the way things begin to take place in your life in a positive way. You have to stay focused on your path that God has you on and if it takes for you to let some things and people go because they are hindering your focus, you have to just let them go. You must pray and get before God and ask God to remove all that's in the way of your focus so that you can be all that God called you to be. Prayer is the most powerful tool that connects you to God and helps you to focus even the more on Him so that you don't be distracted from what He is placing in front of you. When we face obstacles in our life we can tend to lose track of the positive things and lean more to the issues of life. Learn to PRAY and keep your eyes to the hills in which your help comes from because your help comes from the Lord (Psalm 121:1). God can get you back on track with Him and help you move forward pushing you towards destiny. Giving our attention to God will expand many doors that will lead to many blessings because we are putting Him first. The bible tells us that God is a jealous God so this let you know that He is not happy when we are so focused on other things and not Him. This why I encourage you to pray more and gain you attention to God. Just like when you go to work or when you are shopping or when you are doing that you enjoy doing. You will give it your all, this why it is so important to ask our heavenly father to help us be more attentive to the things that matters the most in our lives. Having your prayers be answered by God is an amazing thing because it should draw you closer to Him and that happens because you were setting your heart, mind and soul on Him and Him alone. When you have a solid mindset to do something, nine times out of ten you will do it. We may have other things in this world that we can focus on but one thing is for sure, you can easily be distracted and lose sight of what is more important and that's our purpose in life. Many people now face situations that causes them to get off track and sometimes just plain give up on what it is that they even desired at one point and that's all because of distraction. To me distractions are like poison because it can hit you so quick but hard to get rid of. This why I advise prayer to help push you through difficult times. When you feel like you can't get back in position to finish off where you left off…all you need to do is PRAY and continue to do just that.

This is the one reason I decided to write this book about prayer because I know from experience that it works. Prayer has become part of my lifestyle and my help through life concerning hard and challenging things. I still will continue to go through ups and downs because I'm human just like you. But the great thing about it is that I've learned throughout the years to take things to God and keep my focus on the prize and have faith that everything will be alright. I just want to encourage you that's reading this chapter right now to focus on prayer and begin to put God at the center of your attention. Trust me when I tell you if you do that, watch how God Himself will show you His heart. Prayer is the key to an unlocked door that no man can open but God. All because you made a choice to search for Him and find Him through your focus, you will see Him show Himself to you. Never allow people to take your attention off what God needs you to do. If God need you to pray for other people, then pray for others. If God need you to give people that push in life by ministering to them then do just that. If God need you to encourage others and tell them to have faith in Him then tell them that. The main thing I'm trying to get you to see is that NO ONE is more important than God, focus on Him.

Chapter Seven

THIS TOO SHALL PASS...

*A*s I put my pen to use for this chapter. I think about ALL the trials and situations that God Himself has brought me out. When I think about my life and things I've faced like a situation even now I'm facing concerning my son, I have one son along with 4 beautiful daughter's but my only handsome son that I have is now facing time in prison and this is just to share a little bit of what I deal with of knowing on a daily basis and how each day of my life I'm getting stronger and stronger because I know with God, this all shall pass over. I'm trusting God whole heartedly that my son will be home sooner than the time that was giving to Him. I'm walking in "foolish faith" is what I call it. God said in His good book that, If we will trust Him and believe in His word that we shall have what we believe by faith. I believe that one day I will get my prayers answered concerning my son. Even the situations that you're facing in your own life will pass over one day you just got to believe that God will see you through.

Anything that life presents to us on this earth is only temporarily. Everything has an expiration date on it no matter what it is. Just knowing that God is a way maker and a deliverer of any circumstance to what we face in life. God is ABLE and there is nothing He can't turn around. Just always know that every day is a passing day to go to the next because your trial is passing you by. With prayer and sometimes fasting if needed will help you through hard times. Praying to God is the best thing any of us can do because the answers of our questions is in His hands. Believing that God will bring your prayers to manifestation is an awesome thing because we get to testify about this great and mighty God. I want to encourage you to seek God when you are going through a difficult time because that's when we can reach Him even the more. He knows our hurts, pains and emotions when we are going through. Whatever you are going through today in your life, know that there is nothing too hard for God to push out of the way. Keep your head up and bend on your knees so that you can reach God in prayer. Troubles don't last always (1 Peter 5:10). This chapter is so touching to me because of my son who is facing a situation and it reminds me that what he's facing will pass over one day because as I am a praying mother and who has a passion to pray, I trust God that one day like He did for Peter in the book of Acts, I believe it will be the same results for my son. Also because, I BELIEVE IN THE POWER OF PRAYER! I dedicate this chapter to him and I want to share with you who is reading this right now, something that my son goes by and it's D.UF.F.L.E which stands for something that is encouraging and it is **Don't Underestimate, Face Fears, Live, Elevate**...This is saying, to go forward and don't allow nothing to stop you from being great. I know that better days are ahead and as for you too, You will win! Continue to believe in You and pray about ALL things and watch how God will reveal Himself. It may seem as though God doesn't hear but He does. He pays very close attention to everything. It's nothing that He can't do for you. Your situation doesn't detour your future, it may delay it but it's not denied. This too shall pass and you shall prosper and be stronger than you are now. Keep believing and praying to God and you will see your situation gets better. As your days pass, it is a sign that your trial is coming to an end.

(P.S.) Stay Strong Son,
This too shall pass...
    Y.B
    AKA D.U.F.F.L.E

Long as we keep our faith in God... We will see each day become easier even though it may seem as though it's not getting any better but daily it is getting better. Our trials and tribulations renew our strength each day because with them we wouldn't know that there is a God. God is the one who leads us and holds our hand through hard times. We can move forward and keep pressing to the high calling of Jesus Christ because He alone will see us through the passing of our circumstances. Your great is ahead of you and there is nothing you can't climb over because God is with you always. As you continue to PRAY and build a relationship with Him, He will guide you through and you will pass over your troubles.

Chapter Eight

LEARN TO ENCOURAGE YOURSELF...

*W*hen you are in a difficult place in your life, don't depend on people to always be there in your corner. Everybody you thought would be in your corner when you are facing some hardships in your life is not. It doesn't mean that they should've been because I want to remind you of something, People can't go where God is taking you so therefore there are things and situations you will face is personal. God will allow you to go through obstacles and He will sometimes cause them in your life always because He needs you to build your trust and faith in Him. Many times we as people will run to find somebody to tell our business to far as what we are experiencing but God is trying to get your attention so you can learn to encourage yourself so that you can build up your faith in Him and not mankind. You go before God and pray, I can't stress this enough as I'm writing this book. Read your bible or if you have a devotion that talks about the goodness of the Lord. Getting to know God the more for yourself is all you need to carry you on. Begin to speak declarations over yourself to encourage yourself and your faith. When you speak powerful words like,

I shall live and not die.
I am more than a conqueror in Christ.
I am the head and not the tail.
I am fearfully and wonderfully made.

See when you speak these powerful words over yourself it encourages you to continue because you will feel confident in yourself and knowing that you are responsible for your own encouragement. When there is no one else to uplift your spirits, you must do it on your own. Gain that strength on the inside and declare somethings over your life. Build your own strength and character about you. We are in control of who and what we become because God gave us the power to speak life or death over our self. I want to encourage you to begin to pray over yourself and call positive things out your mouth. Tell yourself that you are prosperous. Say to yourself that you are great. Tell yourself that you are a King or Queen. Tell your-self that you are the child of a powerful God who is in Heaven. Speak positive things over yourself and your life. Words are powerful and what we speak does manifest around us and take root. Also know that words can change your life for the worst or for the better. It depends on you what you become or how you are on this earth. In the bible there is a story about David encouraging himself in the Lord when he was facing a hardship. You see we need that kind of encouragement in our lives. (1 Samuel 30: 6). Even when it looks like nothing will get better, don't go by what you see just believe that your prayers that you pray is being heard by God, because He never falls asleep and His ears are always opened. I want to help you to push and pull through whatever you are going through right now. Rise up and dust yourself off because there is hope and there is truly a God and you can take anything to Him, He will see you through. Prayer will help you reach Him, and you will be strengthened by His presence. I need you this day to build your strength in God and make time for intimacy with the Father so that He can help you in areas where it seems overwhelming. Keep in mind you have a role to play in your life as God develops you in the process. Be encouraged reader.

Chapter Nine

YOUR PRAYERS ARE NOT IN VAIN…

One thing I want you to know is that God hears every prayer that we speak out of our mouths. You've heard the saying before, God hears a sinner's prayer. Our flaws and faults that we create in life does not stop God from hearing us when we pray to Him. But one thing God doesn't like is for us to continue sinning doing the same exact thing and keep asking for Him to forgive us. Don't misunderstand me but He forgives for ALL sins but there is consequences for our wrong doing. We will never do nothing 100% right. It's impossible for us to cross every T and dot every I.

Truth be told we need God's help in everything. Just know that your prayers are NOT in vain. One day or sooner you will see your prayer be answered. I'm a strong believer of our God's glory being manifested because I'm a witness of prayers being answered that I thought He didn't care to hear, yet He answered me.

Don't give up on God because He will never give up on you. A lot of times we think God is not listening when we pray but trust and believe that He hears and He cares. It's in His own perfect timing that He will answer prayers. God knows the right moment and time to move because it will be at the right time and that's when it will be a WOW moment. I can recall when I had this experience while praying to God and though He will not respond to me right now and my prayer was answered quickly than expected. One thing along this journey of my prayer life is that we can't rush God to do nothing! Sometimes He is teaching us lessons that we need to learn from because if He doesn't delay our prayers or prayer then we wouldn't learn how to call upon Him. When praying to God becomes a habit, then you will begin to realize that, long as I'm praying, I know that my Daddy isn't ignoring me because God never sleeps nor slumber.

Always know that God sits high in the heavens and is paying close attention to everything. Your prayers and mine will unlock some blessings and will change some things in our lives that needs work. Continue to seek the Lord and call upon Him while He is near (Isaiah 55: 6). Many of people on this earth life has changed because of their prayers and God heard them. It's times many people don't even believe in God but if you yourself had an experience in your life when you know that it wasn't nobody but God who changed your situation, then that alone should tell you that He hears your prayers. I thank God for who He is in my own life because it was Him who brought me out of dark situations and relationships throughout my life. There was a time in my life when I thought "maybe God isn't listening to me." But the moment He heard me then answered me, it only gave me more Faith to believe in Him. My prayers that I pray are not in vain and I'm so grateful. This why I need you who is reading this book to never give up on PRAYING. God isn't ignoring you, at times He is just waiting for that perfect moment to move. We will tend to be so pushy in prayer but not having enough patience for God to perfect our issues. God knows best for us and it's not that He doesn't hear or isn't listening. There are some things that God wants to protect us from, He knows the ends and outs of life by way of what we can't see. Don't think that God has forgotten about you because He hasn't. Keep drawing near while He is near because WE need God in this life time to see us through. Repent, if you know you have come against the King, He is a forgiving God with arms wide open! The relationship that we build with our daddy in heaven is worth more than anything n the world because it is He that holds our lives in His hands and makes decisions based off our own choices. Listen, if you haven't experienced the presence of God, I advise you to reach out to Him so that you may witness a sweet presence from Him. No prayer is to small or long to reach God, He hears and He understands where you are, but yet He will strengthen you within and pull you close. Don't stop praying and if you haven't started, PLEASE start!

Chapter Ten

YOUR FOOTSTEPS ARE ORDERED BY GOD...

*S*ometimes in our lives we tend to have no direction, but one thing is for certain, that God has already ordered our steps. He has already set out our life as to where we're going. He knows where we will surely end up. I want you to just know that no matter where you are at this point in your life, God has everything figured out for you. Just seek God for guidance and direction so that He can direct your path and you will begin to have clarity and vision. The best thing in life we can do is ask God to show us which way to go and turn because man doesn't always have all the answers. We can go to mom, dad, sister, brother, or even our Pastor's but they don't know 100% what and where God is leading you. The most important thing to do is go to the Lord and ask Him for direction. Even when we take wrong turns in life because of our decision making, just remember that God knows everything and at the end of the day He will turn things around. Your life was already predestined by God and written out in His will. When we tend to do our own thing without consulting God, we end up in some messed up situations that will hinder our blessings and may even hinder our spiritual growth. But thank God that He made it possible for us to come to Him boldly and ask for anything to be moved out of our way that is causing us to walk in the wrong direction. God hears the prayers of those that is faithful in prayer. A bend in the road is not the end of it, just keep moving forward as God is directing your feet to go where He needs them to go. The bible says that the word is a lamp unto my feet and light unto my path (Psalm 119: 105). As long as we read our bible and mediate on what God says, then there is nothing that we can't be saved from when we are going in the right direction. When you are praying ask God to anoint your feet so that you can step into unknown places to receive an unknown blessing. There are some places that God will direct you to go because of a blessing that's waiting for you! I'm grateful that my footsteps are ordered by God, because I don't want to be no place that I shouldn't be. When I'm praying, I ask God to keep my feet from going places they shouldn't go. Order my steps in His word and to teach me, guide me each day. We need our footsteps to be ordered in His word. I pray that this chapter encourages you to ask God to direct your path and to only send you places where His spirit dwells and to keep you from walking in the places where the enemy dwells. May God be your guidance.

Chapter Eleven

KEEP THE FAITH...

*I*n this life We ALL face difficult situations that causes us to feel like God isn't paying attention. One thing I've learned about FAITH is that no matter what you face, God truly knows and sees all. I've experienced some very intense situations in my life that built my strength and my belief. There were times I thought that God was not go pull me through or answer my prayer's but He did. Listen, I can't tell you about having some Faith because the challenges I've been through made me who I am today. I would say: I am a Woman of Faith. I want you to understand that God will come through for you in your most difficult times. I've seen Him do it not just for me but for others that can testify to life and challenges. If only you believe and have a mustard seed of faith, He will move that mountain that's in your way (Luke 17:6). Believe that God can and will do whatever you are believing in Him to do. One thing about our God in heaven, His word is Yes and Amen. He made a promise and He will surely keep it. We can trust God, He's not a liar and will never say something and take it back. I've learned this on my spiritual journey because of prayers that concerned me, my children or love ones and I've watched God's hand move in my prayers. I TRUST GOD!

You may be believing God for a business, job, home, car, relationship connection or anything, but if you just believe and tell God that you know He can do anything but fail, watch Him do it for you because doing what makes us happy is God. We always should desire God's will for our lives because the bible tells us that above ALL things, He wishes that we be in good health and prosper as our souls prosper (3 John 1:2). This should've put a smile on your face just knowing how your God and mines feels about us. Whatever you desire right now, He's able to do it only if you believe in Him. When you pray to God you must take faith, believe and trust with you into His presence. Depending on the source and the creator of ALL things is a big win for you. If any chance you may feel like your prayers are not being answered or heard, it's only because God knows when to answer and how he's going to move. We never want to get ahead of Him because we will delay our prayers. Long as you know that God will and He can, that settles it all because eventually you will see the manifestation of His glory because of your faith. Don't be moved by what you see or what's in front of you, visualize yourself in a positive situation knowing that your prayers will come to past right before your very eyes. My strength has become stronger in faith because of hardships and serious moments that caused me to draw close and closer to God. The moment I believed Him in my hard times was when He showed up and responded So this why I can say to you as I'm sharing how to build your trust in God is because I believed Him before I even prayed. The key to any prayers being answered is FAITH. If we can put trust in humans and believe the word's they say to us, then we should be able to trust God in heaven. I know for some people it's hard to believe in someone unseen but if you have experienced some things along the way and something positive came out of it and you know that mankind couldn't've moved in your situation, but God did! There are some things that you and I can only say God did this! Miracles still are happening on earth and we are a witness to some of them now But, again praying with faith and hope will move the very heart of God to show up in your concerns. One thing is for sure and what I know from experience is that God will never leave you nor will He forsake you. God keeps His promises that He made to you and I and you can always put your trust in Him because He is not like us humans. Your faith will take you to a whole stretch of strength to believe in God. My experience's in life while I'm still growing in God and walking with God, has taught me Faith so strongly! The things that I've been through especially in this year of 2019 has really built my faith and trust in God. There is always something in your life and my life that will teach us how to put our trust and hope in the Lord. One thing about Jehovah God is that our prayers will move Him to answer if only we believe He will do and can do what we are praying for. Be strong and of good courage and know that God is on your side. There is this song that I love so very much because it is encouraging and touching. The name of the song is "Keep the Faith" by Charles Jenkins/ Fellowship Chicago. I encourage you to pull this song up and listen to it, and let it get deep into your spirit and your mind. God is in control of every situation we face, but the bottom line is having faith that God can and He will. No one is exempt from going through the hardships of life. We we're created to glorify God and if it takes trials to come up in our lives just so that God can get our attention and get the glory out of our story, then that's just how it would be. Keep the faith and keep praying!

Chapter Twelve

VICTORY IS YOURS...

*W*hen faced with a battle that you feel is so difficult to conquer, know that God is with you in the midst because anything that we are challenged with on this earth, we must NOT forget that God exist and He doesn't sleep at all. I want you to know that YOU WILL WIN your fight rather it's cancer you are battling or it's a disease in your body that can't be cured, or rather it's financial issues, family situations. It doesn't matter what you go through right now, I want you to know that the battle isn't over unless God says it's over. Speak out your mouth that you will win and believe it when you say it. It's power in our words that we put in the atmosphere. Your challenges come to make you stronger than you are because God is building your faith and equipping you for a finished fight with victory behind it. Just begin to thank God right now where you are in your life and speak "God you created me to be a Winner!" Say this! You are more than a conqueror in Christ Jesus (Romans 8:37) because God created you with strength and power. The devil does exist and that spirit comes to kill, steal, and to destroy us all. This why it's so important to know the word of God because when the devil comes you will know what scripture to fight him with and this is what makes you victorious. Even though Jesus Christ has already won the battle for all of mankind, but we must keep the full Armor of God on and be in the word using our bible. Pray for your strength and endurance because prayer is what strengthens you. We need to acknowledge God in our lives because we need Him to be in the midst of our battles and hard times throughout life. The bible says that one can put 1,000 to flight but two can put 10,000 to flight. When you have a partner with you on the battlefield then you have the victory and your fight will be a strong finish. Continue to fight on and don't give up. You were born to win like I said and long as you believe over doubt then you have already defeated the enemy. Right now where you are I need You to just think a moment about a past situation you was faced with and think about how you didn't know how it will end or how you will overcome it...Look at where you are now, You see how God kept you and brought out? It wasn't nobody but the hand of God on your life. The key thing to it all is that, if PRAYER seems difficult to shake, then you may need to go on a fast and seek the heart of God about what you are praying for.

You have the power and the authority to change things from negative to positive and the reason I say this is because it all depends on us how we respond to a situation or a negative moment. But I say this, Do not allow room to the devil and get in your head to tell you that you can't cross over because he will always try his best to keep you in bondage or captivity. God gave you power over the enemy and to rebuke his lies that he comes with to take you off track and to make you feel like God will not help you. Long as you take my advice and pray, seek God while He can be found then know that you are victorious. Giving up in a battle is not an option. Listen, You and I were created to win and I mean to not walk in defeat. Keep pressing, pushing, praying and holding your head up high because when it's all said and done guess who the winner will be? The winner will be You at the end. If you are currently facing a situation that seems so hard to shake, then I encourage you right now to stop what you're doing and PRAY because God is waiting to answer that urgent prayer. Keep leaning towards God and watch and see how the battle you are facing now will begin to crumble down. Trust God enough to know that He will see you through.

I want to share what PRAYER and FASTING is: Prayer and fasting is defined as voluntarily going without food or whatever you decide to stay away from in order to focus on prayer and fellowship with God. Prayer and fasting often go hand in hand. You can't fast without applying prayer, but when fasting you must attach prayer because you get better results! It's all based on what works for you, just seek God for direction in doing so. But praying and fasting together is more powerful and effective because it's dedicated to God's glory that will cause you to reach God. In doing this it will activate God to answer your heart's desire. Rather, it is simply forcing yourself to focus and rely on God for the strength, provision and wisdom you need. You will see the manifestation of God's power in your life. I need you to transform your mind into a mind of victory because Jesus already won the battle for us and He was victorious. I'm telling you today that "You are Victorious" and you are not defeated! Stay positive and look your situation or mountain in the face and declare your winning season because you are a winner. And always remember that God is always with you when you are faced with a moment of distress. Keep praying and fasting and you will see that situation turn around. Find strength in your dark moments and speak over yourself and tell yourself," I AM" Victorious and Victory is mine! Say it and mean it with faith attached to it and wait on the Lord to back up exactly what you said because He will come through. You are a Winner!

ACKNOWLEDGEMENTS

*F*irst and foremost, I want to Thank God, the headship of my life for giving me the courage to write my 1st book on prayer. I would also like to acknowledge my children, grandson and fiancé for believing in me and for the Woman of God that I am in their lives. I thank God for my Pastor's at New Direction Christian Center, the members and the Deaconess's in this body. To my good friend, my prayer partner, Estella Dior, for encouraging me and helping me push through my disappointments. God has always had His hands on my life and I'm here to say that I am so Grateful for ALL He has done in my life. I must acknowledge the Woman who has been my rock and that's my grandmother Nancy Smith for her prayers and patience with me.

There is someone else that I did not want to miss by any chance and that's Mrs. Wanda Jones who is the parent of my childhood best friend. As a teenager she would get the anointed oil when I would come to her house and anoint me and our other teenage friends and pray over us one by one. I'm grateful for Mrs. Wanda doing this because now that I'm where I am in God, that anointing oil played a major part of my spiritual life outside of my grandmother bringing me up in church as a little girl. But Mrs. Wanda I thank you so much for praying over me when I was young. God Bless you Woman of God. Finally, I want to give thanks to my sister for being who she is in my life. Thanks! Thanks to All.

Encouragement to self...

I AM the giver and not the borrower
I AM Victorious and strong
I AM Unstoppable and not defeated
I AM Blessed and highly favored
I AM healed and whole
I AM God's anointed vessel
I AM a believer in Christ Jesus
I AM Courageous and confident
I AM anointed and very successful
I AM standing on God's word
I AM successful and prosperous
I AM a winner and I will WIN

I just want to encourage you to speak these I AM's over yourself daily and build such a faith within. We must continue to find a way to encourage ourselves and Trust God in doing so. May your I AM's be your reality in Jesus name.

A PRAYER FOR YOU.

*F*or the person who is holding this book in your hands, I pray that God will give you the strength you need to get through your trials and tribulations in your daily life. I pray that God will position you to be a POWERFUL prayer warrior after reading this book. My prayer for you is that God's grace and blessings follows you, your family and those that are dear to your heart everywhere you go! Learn to encourage yourself in the Lord and that you lean on Him and not your own understanding in Jesus name. I pray that when you are weak, in God you are strong. May God quicken your spirit to fast and pray so that you may be drawn to Him. Be of good cheer and know, that God is with you every step of the way and there is nothing hard that He can't fix in your life! (Philippians 4: 6-7).

In Jesus name…Amen.

SYNOPSIS

Porscha Dorsey is an ordained Minister at New Direction Christian Center of Miami Lakes, FL. Gifted with a strong and powerful prayer ministry. She's a volunteer chaplain and has her certificate with National Council for Behavior Health mental health first aid. She has multiple other certificates that explains the prayer call that's on her life. Her family and those that are close in her heart is what gives the drive to her divine purpose. This Woman of God's goal is to draw many people as she can to Jesus Christ through prayer. She believes in the power of Prayer, and this is why she saw fit to encourage and help those that struggles with connecting with God. Her mission is to reach the heart of mankind yet desires for people to build an intimate relationship with God through prayer.

CPSIA information can be obtained
at www.ICGtesting.com
Printed in the USA
LVHW020711310720
661937LV00009BB/273